MICHIGAN

EXPLORE THE UNITED STATES ★ EXPLORE THE UNITED STATES ★ EXPLORE THE UNITED STATES ★

Julie Murray

Big Buddy BOOKS
Explore the United States

VISIT US AT
www.abdopublishing.com

Published by ABDO Publishing Company, PO Box 398166, Minneapolis, MN 55439.

Printed in the United States of America, North Mankato, Minnesota.
042012
092012

♻ PRINTED ON RECYCLED PAPER

Coordinating Series Editor: Rochelle Baltzer
Editor: Sarah Tieck
Contributing Editors: Megan M. Gunderson, BreAnn Rumsch, Marcia Zappa
Graphic Design: Adam Craven
Cover Photograph: *Shutterstock*: Rudy Balasko.
Interior Photographs/Illustrations: *AP Photo*: AP Photo (p. 25), M. Spencer Green (p. 27), North Wind Picture Archives via AP Images (p. 13), Paul Sancya (p. 21); *Getty Images*: Michael P Gadomski/Photo Researchers (p. 30), Getty Images (p. 23), Leon Halip (p. 27); *iStockphoto*: ©iStockphoto.com/HHLtDave5 (p. 19), ©iStockphoto.com/jonathandowney (p. 19), ©iStockphoto.com/Kedward (p. 11), ©iStockphoto.com/Kngkyle2 (p. 9); *Shutterstock*: Thomas Barrat (p. 26), EPG_EuroPhotoGraphics (p. 19), Phillip Lange (p. 30), Doug Lemke (p. 17), Nathaniel Luckhurst (p. 29), Lindsey Moore (p. 27), Dean Pennala (p. 5), Henryk Sadura (p. 9), Michael G Smith (p. 26), Mary Terriberry (p. 30), gregg williams (p. 30).

All population figures taken from the 2010 US census.

Library of Congress Cataloging-in-Publication Data

Murray, Julie, 1969-
 Michigan / Julie Murray.
   p. cm. -- (Explore the United States)
 ISBN 978-1-61783-360-1
 1. Michigan--Juvenile literature. I. Title.
 F566.3.M873 2013
 977.4--dc23
                              2012007059

MICHIGAN

Contents

One Nation

The United States is a **diverse** country. It has farmland, cities, coasts, and mountains. Its people come from many different backgrounds. And, its history covers more than 200 years.

Today the country includes 50 states. Michigan is one of these states. Let's learn more about Michigan and its story!

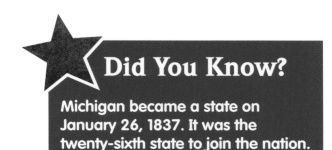

Did You Know?

Michigan became a state on January 26, 1837. It was the twenty-sixth state to join the nation.

Most of Michigan is surrounded by four of the five Great Lakes. These are Lakes Superior, Michigan, Huron, and Erie.

MICHIGAN UP CLOSE

The United States has four main **regions**. Michigan is in the Midwest.

Michigan has three states on its borders. Wisconsin is west. Indiana and Ohio are south. The country of Canada borders Michigan to the east. But, most of Michigan is bordered by water!

Michigan has a total area of 96,713 square miles (250,486 sq km). About 9.9 million people live there.

REGIONS OF THE UNITED STATES

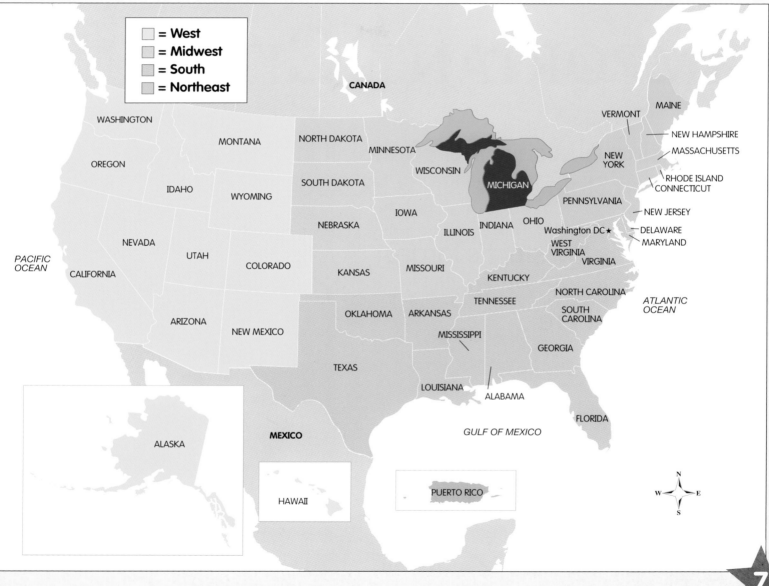

= West
= Midwest
= South
= Northeast

CANADA

WASHINGTON

MONTANA

NORTH DAKOTA

MINNESOTA

WISCONSIN

MICHIGAN

VERMONT

MAINE

NEW HAMPSHIRE

MASSACHUSETTS

OREGON

IDAHO

WYOMING

SOUTH DAKOTA

NEW YORK

RHODE ISLAND
CONNECTICUT

IOWA

PENNSYLVANIA

NEW JERSEY

NEBRASKA

INDIANA

OHIO

Washington DC ★

DELAWARE

MARYLAND

NEVADA

UTAH

ILLINOIS

WEST
VIRGINIA

VIRGINIA

PACIFIC
OCEAN

COLORADO

KANSAS

MISSOURI

KENTUCKY

CALIFORNIA

NORTH CAROLINA

ATLANTIC
OCEAN

TENNESSEE

ARIZONA

NEW MEXICO

OKLAHOMA

ARKANSAS

SOUTH
CAROLINA

MISSISSIPPI

GEORGIA

TEXAS

LOUISIANA

ALABAMA

FLORIDA

ALASKA

MEXICO

GULF OF MEXICO

HAWAII

PUERTO RICO

N
W   E
S

7

IMPORTANT CITIES

Lansing is Michigan's **capital**. It is an **industrial** city. Michigan State University is located nearby in East Lansing.

Detroit is the state's largest city. It is home to 713,777 people. It is known as "Motor City" because many cars are made there.

Michigan

Grand Rapids
Lansing ★
Warren
Detroit

The current Michigan State Capitol is the state's third capitol building.

Detroit is located on the Detroit River. This makes it an important shipping center.

Grand Rapids is Michigan's second-largest city. It is home to 188,040 people. Many products are made in this **industrial** city.

Warren is the state's third-largest city. It has 134,056 people. This city is part of the Detroit **metropolitan** area. Many cars and car parts are made there.

Grand Rapids is located on the Grand River.

MICHIGAN IN HISTORY

Michigan's history includes Native Americans and settlers. Native Americans have lived in present-day Michigan for thousands of years. In about 1620, a French explorer visited the area. Over time, the French claimed and settled the land. In 1701, Detroit was founded. People traded goods there.

By 1783, the United States controlled the Michigan area. A waterway called the Erie Canal was finished in 1825. Then, boats could easily reach Michigan from the east. So, more people began moving there. In 1837, Michigan became a state.

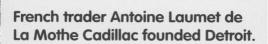

French trader Antoine Laumet de
La Mothe Cadillac founded Detroit.

13

Timeline

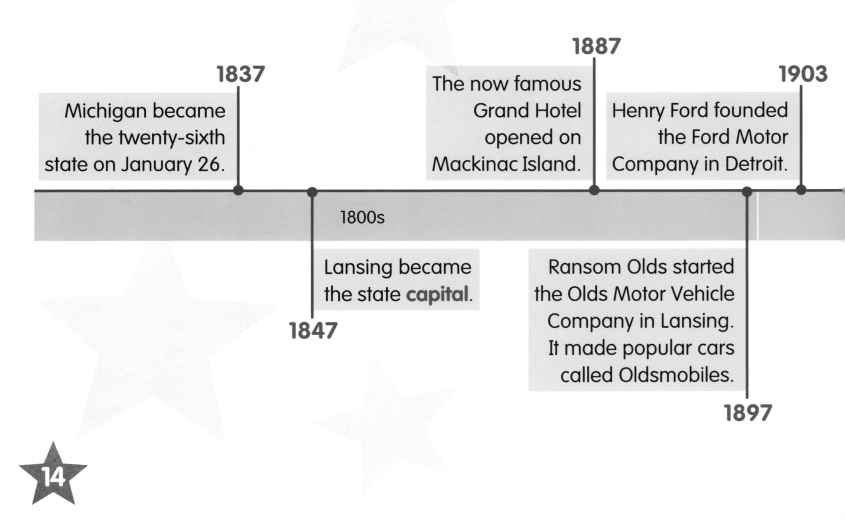

1837

Michigan became the twenty-sixth state on January 26.

1887

The now famous Grand Hotel opened on Mackinac Island.

1903

Henry Ford founded the Ford Motor Company in Detroit.

1800s

1847

Lansing became the state **capital**.

1897

Ransom Olds started the Olds Motor Vehicle Company in Lansing. It made popular cars called Oldsmobiles.

1929

The first Tulip Time Festival was held in Holland, Michigan. The city grew 100,000 tulips!

1974

Gerald Ford of Grand Rapids became the thirty-eighth US president.

2008

The Detroit Red Wings hockey team won their eleventh Stanley Cup.

1900s

2000s

Berry Gordy Jr. started Motown Records in Detroit. Motown grew famous for hit music by African-American singers. These included Diana Ross and Stevie Wonder.

1959

More than 800,000 gallons (3 million L) of oil spilled in the Kalamazoo River near Marshall. It was one of the Midwest's worst oil spills.

2010

15

ACROSS THE LAND

Michigan is divided into two parts by Lake Michigan. The land north of the lake is called the Upper **Peninsula**. In the west, it has rocky hills, mountains, and cliffs. In the east, it has low **swamps**. The land east of the lake is called the Lower Peninsula. It has sand **dunes**, rolling hills, and farmland.

Many types of animals make their homes in Michigan. These include deer, bears, ducks, turkeys, and moose. Whitefish and trout are found in the Great Lakes.

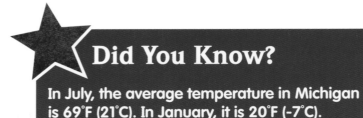

Did You Know?

In July, the average temperature in Michigan is 69°F (21°C). In January, it is 20°F (-7°C).

Many parts of Michigan have forests.
The state also has about 11,000 lakes.

EARNING A LIVING

Michigan is known for farming and **industry**. Farms produce fruits, vegetables, and dairy. Many factories make automobiles and metal products.

Michigan is a popular vacation spot. So, many people have jobs helping visitors. Other people work in mines. The state provides **limestone**, gravel, and sand.

Michigan is a top grower of apples (*above*), blueberries (*right*), cherries, and peaches.

Sports Page

Many people think of sports when they think of Michigan. Detroit teams play baseball, hockey, basketball, and football.

College sports are also popular in the state. The University of Michigan is known for football. And, Michigan State University is known for basketball.

The Detroit Tigers play baseball at Comerica Park.

HOMETOWN HEROES

Many famous people are from Michigan. Henry Ford was born in Wayne County in 1863. He is known for making cars.

In 1903, Ford started the Ford Motor Company. In 1908, he created the Model T. Ford found a way to build the Model T faster and cheaper than other cars. So, this was one of the first cars that many people could afford.

Ford helped change the way Americans traveled!

Charles Lindbergh was born in Detroit in 1902. He was famous for flying airplanes.

In 1927, Lindbergh made the first nonstop one-person airplane flight across the Atlantic Ocean! He flew from New York City, New York, to Paris, France, in 33.5 hours.

Lindbergh made his famous flight on the *Spirit of St. Louis.*

Tour Book

Do you want to go to Michigan? If you visit the state, here are some places to go and things to do!

 **See**

Visit the city of Holland in May for the Tulip Time Festival. It is one of the largest US flower festivals!

 **Visit**

Spend time on Mackinac Island. No cars are allowed there. Instead, you can walk, bike, or ride in horse-drawn carriages. Stop by the historic Grand Hotel!

⭐ Remember

Visit the Gerald R. Ford Museum in Grand Rapids. There, you can learn about Ford, who was president from 1974 to 1977. Ford grew up in Grand Rapids and went to the University of Michigan.

⭐ Cheer

Catch a University of Michigan versus Michigan State University game. It is exciting to see these rivals play football, basketball, and other sports!

⭐ Discover

Tour Pictured Rocks National Lakeshore on Lake Superior. It is known for multicolored rock. Sandstone cliffs rise up to 200 feet (61 m) above the water.

A GREAT STATE

The story of Michigan is important to the United States. The people and places that make up this state offer something special to the country. Together with all the states, Michigan helps make the United States great.

Mackinac Bridge connects Michigan's Upper and Lower Peninsulas. It is 8,344 feet (2,543 m) long!

Fast Facts

Date of Statehood:
January 26, 1837

Population (rank):
9,883,640
(8th most-populated state)

Total Area (rank):
96,713 square miles
(11th largest state)

Motto:
"Si Quaeris Peninsulam
Amoenam Circumspice"
(If You Seek a Pleasant
Peninsula, Look About You)

Nickname:
Wolverine State,
Great Lake State

State Capital:
Lansing

Flag:

Flower: Apple Blossom

Postal Abbreviation:
MI

Tree: White Pine

Bird: American Robin

30

Important Words

capital a city where government leaders meet.

diverse made up of things that are different from each other.

dune a hill or ridge of loose sand piled up by the wind.

industry the process of using machines and factories to make products.

limestone a type of white rock used for building.

metropolitan of or relating to a large city, usually with nearby smaller cities called suburbs.

peninsula land that sticks out into water and is connected to a larger piece of land.

region a large part of a country that is different from other parts.

swamp land that is wet and often covered with water.

Web Sites

To learn more about Michigan, visit ABDO Publishing Company online. Web sites about Michigan are featured on our Book Links page. These links are routinely monitored and updated to provide the most current information available.

www.abdopublishing.com

Index